THIS BOOK BELONGS TO

Made in the USA
Monee, IL
26 September 2022

14700632R00070